Dear Pastors and Traveling Ministers,

Harold R. Eberle

Winepress Publishing
Yakima, Washington

Dear Pastors and Traveling Ministers,
A Handbook to Help Pastors and Traveling Ministers
Relate and Minister Together Effectively

© 1998 by Harold R. Eberle

Winepress Publishing
PO Box 10653, Yakima, WA 98909-1653 USA

First printing, June 1998

Library of Congress Catalog Card No. 98-090361
ISBN 1-882523-10-5

Unless otherwise noted, all biblical quotations are taken from the New American Standard Bible, © 1960, 1962, 1963, 1968, 1971, 1972, 1973, 1975, 1977 by the Lockman Foundation. Used by permission.

Cover by Angela Hopkins
Graphic work by Eugene Holmes

Printed in the United States of America

Inquiries about translating into other languages should be addressed to Winepress Publishing.

Thanks and Dedication

My special thanks go to Pastors Mike and Nancy Prato who inspired me to write this book and have stood with me over the last few years. Dennis Jacobson, Peter Eisenmann, and Annette Bradley helped with the editing process.

This book is dedicated to the pastors who put up with me while I made so many mistakes during my earlier years traveling in the ministry.

Table of Contents

Introduction

In 1980 my wife and I began pastoring our first church. It was successful by most "church standards" but during those first six years we went through the blessings and heartbreaks every pastor experiences. After a visitation of the Lord in 1986, I left the pastorate and began traveling in order to minister to the larger Body of Christ. I have been on the road ever since, with the exception of an eight-month period during which I tried to escape the traveling ministry and settled down to pastor a second church. I must admit—aside from the lessons God taught me—that church was not successful. I went back on the road ministering, and after four years of struggling, God started blessing our labors greatly. Although we are well-accepted now, it has been a long hard road.

Perhaps I can help some other ministers smooth out their path.

This book is meant to be a manual to help pastors and traveling ministers (TMs) work together. I hope I can address some key areas with a perspective from both sides. Not only have I

Dear Pastors and Traveling Ministers,

lived on both sides but I have relationships with hundreds of pastors today and dozens of TMs. I hear their concerns and have a heart to make things work effectively in the Body of Christ. Let's see if we can communicate.

In some of the chapters, I have addressed the pastors and the TMs separately. In other chapters I deal with the issues together. Please read it all or turn to a subject in which you are interested.

I will be using the abbreviation TM to stand for traveling minister. Also I will be using the male gender to refer to pastors and TMs, although I accept and believe fully in women in the ministry. Please do not think that I am preferring one gender over another. Finally, let me say that I refer to the senior minister of a local church as a "pastor." This is the most commonly accepted title, but people who know me personally realize that I believe in the full five-fold ministry—apostles, prophets, evangelists, pastors, and teachers (Eph. 4:11).

Chapter 1

Scheduling

To the Pastors,

How often should you invite TMs to come to your church?

Every stream of Christianity is structured differently. The mega-churches typically have several qualified ministers on staff, and there is little opportunity or need (except for special conferences) for outsiders to come and minister. Some churches belong to denominations which limit guest speakers to a specific number, or to those licensed within that denomination. Most, however, leave such decisions to either the senior minister or board of directors.

Personally, I like to see a local church invite an outside speaker to the Sunday morning service about every six to eight weeks. It is healthy for the church to have an outsider stand behind the pulpit on Sunday morning, confirming the work of the local minister and stirring the people to godliness. It is good to have two or three regular, trusted TMs come at least once a year, and it is also good to introduce some fresh life to your people now and then.

In addition to the above-mentioned guest visits on Sunday mornings, a healthy church can also host two, three, or more special conferences during the year. Guest speakers can be brought in for a weekend conference, or for a series of meetings on a special topic which the senior minister determines would be helpful for his people.

Now please do not take this as a legalistic rule. There are all kinds of churches and the local pastor must decide what is best for his flock. I simply am suggesting these time periods because pastors sometimes ask me what I think is healthy. What is healthy is what the pastor decides is healthy. I am simply telling you what I often have seen work in churches.

There are some churches which are "convention-oriented." They build their ministry around incoming speakers. Most medium and large-sized cities have at least one church like this, and God blesses them. There can be considerable excitement and growth around a ministry structured like this. I would caution such churches, however, to make available some type of small group interaction. Also, extra attention needs to be given to pastoral care, as it often gets neglected. Even in the convention-oriented church, the people need to have established, stable, long-term leadership whom they can trust at the forefront.

Whom should you invite to speak at your church?

Do not arrange for speakers you do not know. Sometimes pastors schedule TMs out of a sense of guilt or obligation. They know they should allow outside ministers to speak to their people, but perhaps they have not built relationships with any. Or someone has recommended an unknown TM to the pastor, and the pastor felt pressured into making room for the outsider. Mistake! It is the senior minister's responsibility to protect his sheep. A visiting minister standing in the pulpit with charisma on his life can have tremendous influence on a congregation. Many churches have been hurt by the visit of an unknown speaker. Don't let that happen.

At the first church I pastored, I had about ten different TMs speak to my congregation. With the exception of two, our church experienced both blessings and edification from each speaker. The two exceptions were men of God trying their best to please the Lord, but their emphasis differed so much from my own that it caused confusion among the congregation. It took me two or three weeks afterward to straighten out the mess.

A senior minister always must be confident enough to correct teaching that contradicts what he believes. Of course, there are many smaller emphases in Christianity that can be discussed without causing any turmoil. The average congregational member should be mature enough to "eat the meat and spit out the bones." However, they need to be so informed. Because people sometimes respect and even reverence a certain

TM, they may receive all he says without discernment. Christians need to be told by their pastor that all things should be judged according to the Word of God.

I do not want to put fear in people, and I personally would not want to minister to a crowd where everyone is on the defensive from the start. I simply am saying that the senior minister of any congregation must not let down his responsibility of watching out for his flock.

After a TM has built relationships with a certain congregation and has established a proven track record, then the local minister can and will trust him, and a wonderful relationship can proceed.

When contacting a TM for the first time, it is important that communication is clear. In Appendix A of this book I have inserted a sample questionnaire that can be completed by the TM and given to you for your information. In response, you can answer the questions on the form in Appendix B. You will be amazed at how simple questions can make a visit much more pleasant for both parties.

In order to prevent conflicts or bad feelings, you should discuss financial arrangements in advance. Most TMs with whom I work have no specific requirements, but a few do.

If you have a small congregation and it would be difficult for you to take care of a certain TM financially, then you can offer to make arrangements for him to speak at several churches in your area. Many TMs greatly appreciate such an offer, and more likely will come, knowing that expenses will be shared. However, if you are bringing in a speaker just to your congregation, be ready and willing to cover costs and bless their work.

In Chapter 4 of this book, we discuss financial concerns in greater detail.

Sometimes it is difficult to get TMs—especially the well-known ones—to visit the smaller churches. Allow me to let you in on a secret. We would like to think that "men and women of God" hear His voice and go where the Spirit leads, but in actuality they respond to certain cues. Number one is hunger. The TMs that I know all love to minister to people who desperately desire to receive from them. Let's face it—most TMs appreciate being appreciated. If you, therefore, express your respect and desire for the TM you wish to invite, he will be more likely to come. Pull on their heart, rather than on their pocketbook. Write a pleading letter; tell them how much your people need their ministry; telephone more than once; leave messages; make your request stand out. Win them and they will come.

How far in advance should you schedule? The bigger the church, the farther ahead planning must be made. Similarly, the more in demand a speaker is, the farther in advance you must make arrangements. In churches with over a thousand people, I find that I need to schedule a year in advance. Churches under 300 usually schedule three months to a year ahead. Churches under 100 usually think one month in advance.

Once you have confirmed a schedule, do not break your commitment. This can be a serious offense in the eyes of the TM. They probably have arranged other meetings in your area, turned down requests from pastors in other regions, and been praying for your meetings. To have a pastor cancel is one of the most difficult things TMs experience. I have been at several dinners with TMs and heard their sad stories of pastors who let them down after they made extensive plans. It may seem small from your side to cancel a meeting, but it is major for a TM.

To the Traveling Ministers,

Scheduling meetings is one of the most trying responsibilities for most TMs. Before they started in the ministry, they envisioned themselves standing in front of people, preaching—not doing administrative work and spending extended periods on the phone. There is a saying among TMs: "Unless you are the son of somebody famous, the door to the pastor's office is closed, but there is a crack under the door big enough for your book or tape." It is true that getting started in a traveling ministry can be very difficult, and most do not succeed. Once a person has become well-known, it is easy to schedule meetings, because requests come in constantly. However, when no one knows who you are, the phone doesn't ring.

What can be done to schedule meetings? Here are several suggestions.

One well-known Christian leader said, "The convention is the grocery store for the traveling minister." By this we mean that pastors and other leaders come together at conventions and many key relationships begin there. The wise TM will take advantage of such opportunities to network and "go shopping." It is not a matter of just handing out one's business cards and introducing oneself. It takes more than that. Relationships must be built. Therefore, you need to attend Christian conventions and take every opportunity to have breakfast, lunch, dinner, or coffee with leaders who pastor churches. Be a friend. Share your heart and vision if the occasion arises. Sit in the congregation and be a part. Rub shoulders. But between meetings, work.

Relationships also can be made outside the convention setting. I began in the traveling ministry by driving my car to a town, telephoning any minister I could find and asking him if I could get together with him for coffee or a meal. I built many relationships this way.

One of the door openers I have discovered is personal prophecy. By this I mean, I stay open to the leading of the Lord to see if He will give me a word of prophecy for that minister. Beware that some ministers receive too much unwelcome prophecy, and they may not want to hear from a stranger. However, if God has given you a gift along these lines, realize that prophecy is a sign to believers (I Cor. 14:22); that is why God gave us the gift. If you prophesy an accurate word to a leader, it will be a sign to them that God is certainly with you. Again and again I have seen pastors ask me if I will come and minister to their people after I ministered to them.

It does not have to be prophecy: prayer or a listening ear both work as well.

An additional way to touch their lives is to minister alongside another TM who is willing to open the door for you. For example, if you have a relationship with a certain TM and that individual is ministering somewhere, go and sit in the meeting. If God allows, that TM may ask you to come up to the front and help pray over people at the end of the service. Or the traveling friend may simply ask you to join with the other leaders for dinner after the service. I have opened the door for several TMs into other churches and they have opened doors to me. TMs need to work together.

Of course, you should not get yourself entangled with another TM who has a bad reputation. A good name is a great asset (Prov. 22:1), and you can ruin yours by hanging around the wrong people. I am not saying only to hobnob with the successful. I am merely pointing out that care must be taken, because your associations reflect your character.

For the most part, sending out letters which

introduce yourself to pastors will not open any doors for you. It takes a personal, face-to-face contact. And that is the way it should be. Pastors have God-given responsibilities to guard their sheep, and they are fools to let just anyone minister to their people. I have seen several "wannabes" try to get started in the ministry by mailing out introductory letters to all the pastors for whom they could find addresses—none of them succeeded that way—including myself. Of course, an introductory letter can help introduce your name, but it will still take your personal presence before leaders will trust you with their sheep.

Perhaps the most important scheduling advice I give to TMs is, "Carry a pocket-sized calendar everywhere you go and plan ahead." This cannot be emphasized enough. If and when a pastor says, "Maybe we can have you come and minister sometime," you must immediately be there with a response. Do not let it pass for even a second. The next words that should come out of your mouth are, "Well, I will be coming through your area on such and such a time; I would love to minister to your people then." Take out your calendar while you are saying those words, and offer a specific time period.

Realize that to be ready for scheduling, you always must be thinking ahead. The bigger the church, the farther ahead you have to plan. If a pastor of a thousand people asks you to come and minister, don't say that you are free next week-

end. He could not have such a large church
unless he was a man of far-reaching vision. He is
probably thinking several months ahead, and if
you want to fit into his plans, you must get on his
wave length. Always have in your mind a time
you can come several months or even a year
down the road. Even if you really are free next
weekend, don't tell him that, because you will
look like a fool! Get your act together and think
long-range. Plan a year at a time.

A traveling minister without a calendar in
his pocket is like a carpenter without a hammer,
a cook without a pan, a secretary without a
phone, a pilot without a plane, or an idiot without
his head.

The best time to schedule a meeting is immediately after ministering at a meeting. A local
pastor almost always will ask you back to minister again if your ministry was a blessing to his
church. Or if there is a visiting minister sitting in
the congregation while you are speaking, he is
most likely to come up and ask you to come to his
church. Before you leave that pastor's presence,
you must pull out your calendar and suggest a
date when you can come back. Do not say, "I will
call you in a week to schedule another time." In a
week the excitement is over. They have gone on
with their life. The one dissatisfied person in the
congregation who did not like you has complained to the pastor. You are history. You must
—I said you must—reschedule before you leave
the presence of the pastor. It is also a safeguard

for yourself, because it keeps the pastor's heart directed and committed to you for the future.

The traveling ministry is business. Yes, it is God's business, but it is still business.

You must look at this as a business which you can build. Do not think you will succeed by hitting a church one time and then never coming back. Instead, think of relationship-building. Every church you go to is an ongoing relationship which you can visit, once or twice (perhaps more) each year.

If you approach it this way, you can realize that you only need relationships with a handful of pastors to succeed. For example, if you aim at ministering at each church twice per year, you only need 26 churches in order to have every Sunday scheduled for the rest of your life. Now, I do not mean to make this sound so mechanical, because, obviously, God will have you moving around, growing into new relationships, and expanding. However, I want you to see how easy it really can be if you very practically and simply set out to build relationships with a few pastors. No one told me this when I started out. Instead, I thought I would be breaking into new, antagonistic territory every day for the rest of my life. It was difficult getting those first meetings, and if I'd had to continue working that hard, my family would have starved a long time ago. Today, I have constant requests from churches, but back when I was starting out, I did not have any success until I began to think in terms of building and maintaining relationships. That is the way things work.

Once a base of churches—say 26—has been established, you can start expanding your ministry. I like to go on weekend trips if they are within driving distance, or ten-day trips if I have to fly to another region. In ten days I can cover two Sundays and usually minister to several churches in the area during the weekday evenings. Longer than ten days away and I miss my family too much.

While on trips, I also like to get together with local pastors during the daytime for breakfast, lunch, dinner, or leadership meetings. I make it my goal to touch bases with all the pastors in an area with whom I already have relationships, and I like to pioneer new areas constantly. Even if a certain congregation is small and secluded, I like to be adding new people into whose lives I can input.

No meeting should be considered insignificant. Of course, all people are important and deserve our best ministry. But it is also true that every door—even a seemingly insignificant door—is another door. A famous TM told me this when I was first starting out on the road, and sure enough, I have discovered it to be true. Even if you are ministering to a group of four people in the living room of a home, there is probably someone there who knows someone of influence, and they will open a bigger door for you in the future. Of course, we should be happy to minister where God has called us, so if you find yourself ministering only in small groups for years, do not get discouraged.

Keep in mind that you will grow with the people to whom you minister. Year by year you will be refining your gifts and abilities. I look back at the things I used to teach and the manner in which I ministered, and I am so glad that God did not put me in front of big crowds back then. I did not know it then, but I was not ready. Not only have I matured over the years, but so have the people. Some of the pastors who ten years ago had only a handful of people, now have substantial-sized churches. Influential people often come up to me and tell me that I prophesied or prayed over them years ago when they were sitting in some small meeting in a forgotten community. Every relationship is a future door. Think this way.

Right now there are thousands of churches out there wanting and needing people to come and minister. In a small town of say 40,000 people, there may be as many as a hundred churches. Of course, many of them belong to denominations that allow only their own ministers to speak, and others are so large that only the famous, well-established speakers will get in. However, about 50 of those 100 churches are wishing for outside input. Multiply that 50 by all the number of cities in the country and your eyes will open up to the amount of work out there. But you must begin by opening the door to the first few pastors—build relationships with them and become the kind of person pastors can trust (more about that last requirement as we continue).

Chapter 2

Ethical Concerns with Gender

The TM should never be alone with a person of the opposite sex unless it is a member of his own family. This is a good rule for both pastors and TMs, but the traveling ministry presents some unique situations in this regard.

One situation which commonly arises is that the person assigned to give transportation to the TM from the airport to a motel, or from a motel to the meeting location, is a church secretary (or the spouse of the local minister). When it is across genders, this is a mistake. Most of the churches where I minister know that I do not want to be placed in such a position (unless my wife is with me).

It is not necessarily that I will fall into sin, although I am a human with frailties as anyone else. It is more an issue of *improperly bonding* with individuals of the opposite sex. It is a fact that men and women communicate differently. They share their hearts in different ways. God has created men and women to complement and meet each other's needs. Because a TM typically has some amount of authority upon his life, it is easy for the local leaders to share their hearts and jump at the opportunity to talk. Of course, this is of great benefit, and sharing the trials and struggles of local ministry with a trusted outside authority can be wonderful. However, when a man and woman have an occasion to share their hearts with one another, they commonly bond with each other. Such bonding can violate husband/wife relationships. When individuals share their hearts with outsiders on a deeper level than they share their hearts with their spouse, the door for problems is being opened. Don't do it. Even though it may feel right and helpful at the time, it is a trap.

Bonding which violates healthy relationships also can occur when people of the opposite sex minister together for any length of time. For example, I often speak in foreign countries, and when I minister through an interpreter, I discover a closeness that quickly develops between me and that individual. Therefore, I do not want my interpreter to be a person of the opposite sex—it is neither fair to my wife nor to the female interpreter.

Even praying together can open the door for unhealthy bonding. When I have people who need prayer at the end of a meeting, I do not touch the women, except for brief moments upon the forehead or shoulders—especially if the female is anywhere near my age. If there is an illness and I sense that hands should be laid on another part of a woman's body, I will ask a female leader—usually my wife or the pastor's wife—to come and lay hands on the person needing prayer.

I am concerned not only about improper contact with the woman for whom I am praying, but also with females who may minister with me. Spiritual ministry is incredibly intimate and can open the door for deep bonding. When a man and woman stand together and pray, preach, prophesy, or exercise any other spiritual gifts together, they easily may become "of one mind and heart." It can lead to problems weeks, months, and years down the road. Not only does it create bonds between the two, but it can intrude upon the relationships which both already have established with their spouses.

Of course, if my wife is present, there is a safeguard. Women are especially sensitive to improper bonding, and a wife usually knows exactly where her husband's heart is. Therefore, I trust my wife, but when I am ministering somewhere without her, I am especially careful and perhaps even stand-offish toward women.

I can't emphasize this enough. Many times I have had sweet little women come up to me at the end of a meeting and ask for prayer. They may honestly be thinking that prayer is what they need, but their own need for a man's attention also can have something to do with their request.

Be careful in a crowd and completely avoid situations alone with a person of the opposite sex.

Of course, part of this is simply for the purpose of avoiding the appearance of evil. This point can sound trite to some, and certain individuals would mock this caution, claiming that it is no one else's business with whom they are riding in a car or visiting alone. Please do not think that. Billy Graham and his staff made it a practice to never be alone with a person of the opposite sex, and setting that standard helped establish an integrity that won the respect of millions. The more well-known a person becomes, the more important this issue becomes. People on the street, in the local grocery store, stopped at an intersection, or at the gas station recognize influential leaders. If someone attending a certain meeting innocently runs into the speaker as he or she is being transported to the meeting by a person of the opposite sex, rumors can start. This is especially true if that individual finds an occasion at a later time to dislike the TM. Memories of a TM with a person of the opposite sex can be blown out of proportion.

Whether or not, there is any substance to an accusation, it can cause damage. It is not worth risking one's ministry.

To take this one step further, I expect TMs with whom I work to keep the door closed as much as possible to wrong relationships with the opposite sex. For example, a married minister should wear a wedding ring when he is standing in the pulpit. There is a charismatic presence that typically settles on a speaker up front, and that presence can make an individual appear more attractive than they look at other times. Lonely individuals of the opposite sex sitting in the audience too easily can give themselves over to vain imaginations. A ring boldly displayed is a shield. Even better is for the minister to make regular mention of his spouse, along with any children he has.

When I pastored, I once had a TM speak at our church, but he was not wearing a ring nor mentioning his wife at anytime. I took the opportunity at an evening meal to discuss the dangers, and he appreciated the comments I made—at least I think he did. But it does not matter, because whether or not he appreciated them, he needed to hear, and as a pastor watching over a flock, I needed to address the issue.

Chapter 3

Traveling Minister and Congregational Member Relationships

A recurring point of contention has to do with relationships which TMs sometimes develop with members of a congregation, aside from the leadership. Of course, we want TMs to be cordial to all members, and we want them to build into the lives of the people. However, there are some relationships which can be destructive to a local congregation.

For example, in most congregations there are a few individuals who are at odds with the direction the church presently is going and, hence, are frustrated with the senior minister. Too often those individuals will seek out the opinion, advice, judgment, or support of a visiting minister. Because they find themselves being rejected in their viewpoint, they want reassurance from a person whom they respect. We cannot blatantly condemn individuals for seeking such support. It is natural to want reassurance, however, we must be wise in how to handle the problems which can result.

When a frustrated individual contacts me to express his dissatisfaction with the local church leadership, the first thing I want to do is tell him to talk to his leaders. Otherwise, I want to excuse myself from the conversation. I have seen this situation too often lead to greater conflict.

The Bible clearly tells us not to receive an accusation against an elder except on the basis of two or three witnesses. If a report of sexual or serious financial misconduct arises, I may choose to investigate further. Or if I do not have the appropriate relationship with that specific church, I may pass the report on to the appropriate leaders.

However, the vast majority of conflicts pertain to the senior minister guiding the church in a different direction than the frustrated person desires. Such issues are easily settled: The senior minister is right and the congregational member is wrong! That is the definition of the senior minister—lead. That is his job.

Another common complaint is that the senior minister will not allow a certain individual to use his gifts in the church. I have met many people who think they are anointed for some ministry, but in reality they do not bless me. I hate to be the one to tell them that they simply are not anointed, and I do not feel as if I should be involved in such conflicts, anyway. If, indeed, it is a person who has a valid gift, but the senior minister is not allowing him to express it, I still would prefer to tell the individual that it is an issue to be resolved between him and his pastor.

This may sound hard and cold, but in such conflicts it is difficult, as an outsider, to accomplish anything beneficial. No matter what you say, it can and usually will be turned around to your harm. If you as a TM encourage the individual in his gifts, sooner or later he may throw your words in the face of the senior minister. Then you are made to look like the bad guy. If, on the other hand, the TM discourages the person from ministry, it may be contrary to the very purposes of God for that individual. Typically, the TM who comes in for just a glimpse of the local dynamics in a church does not have enough information to give wise counsel on such issues. If, indeed, the senior minister is holding a certain person back, there is probably a reason. Pastors are smart. They are gifted by God to lead a congregation. It is their job. TMs, let the pastor do it. Stay out of it.

If someone from a certain congregation telephones a TM at home in order to complain about his pastor, what should be done? First of all, I do not like such calls, and I avoid them as much as possible. At the risk of appearing hard and uncaring, I am usually "not home." If a TM does get trapped in a corner where complaints are spilling forth, he can say, "You need to realize that I have a relationship with your pastor, and I will have to contact him and talk to him about what you are saying as soon as we finish speaking!" Such words will bring a sobriety to the conversation.

Even a relationship which is not complaint-based between a TM and a congregational member can cause difficulties in the local congregation. Too often the congregational member begins looking to the TM as his or her final authority in all spiritual matters. The pastor then can no longer pastor that person. It is terribly frustrating for a pastor to be told again and again that a certain TM believes differently or would do things differently. By saying this, we are not condemning all such relationships. We simply want TMs to see the problem from the local pastor's perspective and, hence, to take precautions.

Allow me to emphasize this last point by sharing with you a hard realization to which I came during my years on the road. As a traveling minister, it is easy to get people to love you. It is rewarding to have them look to your leadership. However, a form of spiritual adultery often takes place in such relationship dynamics.

One time I was visiting with a man who had spent several years in prison for murder. He had paid his debt to society, but he confided in me of other sins related to an earlier lifestyle given to adultery. He had seduced several married women. He mentioned that all he did was take a little time to treat married women better than their husbands did, and soon they would go to bed with him. This struck me.

Some time later my wife and I watched a movie which portrayed a man who worked as a traveling photographer. His career seemed exciting as he could see the sights of the world and be free to *do* whatever and *go* wherever he desired. Then he came across a married woman who felt trapped in a humdrum lifestyle of raising a family. The photographer gave her the attention for which she longed and which her husband was not giving her. He spoke of the exciting places he had been and drew a picture in her mind of a freedom of which she had not dreamed since she was a young single woman. He noticed her talents and gifts. He expressed belief in her abilities. In just a short time, her heart turned away from her husband and fixed on him. Soon he moved on to other places, but her heart remained pointed toward him, and she was estranged from her husband for the rest of her life.

When I saw that movie, I determined that I would not be like the photographer, tantalizing lonely Christians who faithfully are serving in a local church, yet inwardly are longing for a more exciting lifestyle.

In this light, consider the proper relationship a TM should have with a congregation. Some TMs who have been in the ministry for years often seem distant or even unfriendly to the people. Many walk onto the church platform after the music has begun and quickly disappear at the end of the service. In the minds of the onlooker, it sometimes seems as if the speaker is arrogant and aloof. It even can cause the Christians sitting in the pews to mistrust that person.

Some TMs, indeed, may be conducting themselves that way because they do not care about
the people, or they may be very busy running
from one meeting to another. Of course, I am not
making excuses for that or any self-exalting posi-
tioning. Nor am I encouraging ministers to be
distant from the people. I just am cautioning the
TMs not to play with the hearts of God's people
and lead them away from their church home.

Chapter 4

Financial Matters

We hope and believe that both pastors and TMs serve God primarily out of a motivation to please Him and to answer the calling upon their lives. However, money is important, and serious offenses arise from the misuse of finances.

To the Pastors,

Please realize that most TMs depend upon the gift your church gives in order to support their families and further ministry. Some TMs travel from church to church and minister several times every week. However, most jump from weekend to weekend, with an occasional weekday service. If they have only four Sunday meetings in a month, the offering they receive from your church will be one-fourth of their support that month. Consider what that means. If they receive a small offering, say $500 from your church, and the same amount from each of the other three churches, they will have only $2000 come in that month. You also should realize that only about half of that amount will end up in the hands of the TM. The rest will be required for travel, office, and ministry expenses. Is it any wonder that of the thousands of sincere Christians who attempt to succeed in traveling ministry, very few survive?

From my own experiences beginning on the road, I can tell you that I slept in my car many, many nights during the first four years. My wife, who was home with the three children, says the most difficult times were not when there was no food, but when there was no toilet paper. Been there! Done that!

Once a TM has become established and well-accepted, the financial dynamics change greatly. They may have a large mailing list and individuals supporting their ministry, income from the sales of books and tapes, or churches supporting them on a regular basis. However, the well-known ones have tremendous responsibilities and financial commitments of their own. They may have a large staff managing an office and commitments to support ministries in many third-world countries. Established ministries have "sharp-pencil" administrators who know how much income must be generated. Therefore, to have one come to your church typically requires thousands of dollars. Usually, hosting a well-known speaker is best left to the large convention where many churches are coming together.

I am hoping here to give advice on how to

help the TM who works more on a smaller scale, wanting to minister in your church, perhaps alone or with one or two staff members.

How much should you pay? When you make initial contact with the TM, you should ask if they have a set amount which they charge. A few have figured their costs and will tell you openly. Most, however, will come and minister on the basis "of faith," believing that God will provide, while hoping you will be fair toward them. What is fair? You pay for their traveling expenses, plus a love offering. The traveling expenses should *not* be paid out of the offering received for the speaker. They should be covered by the church and assumed as the cost of ministry. The love offering is in addition to the traveling cost.

If the TM flies into your area, you should offer to buy their ticket or to refund them the cost. If they drive, you should have an open discussion and say, "We want to cover your costs, plus bless you with a love offering. It would help us to know what your travel expenses are."

A smaller church which cannot afford a certain TM can offer to schedule him at other nearby churches and, therefore, share the traveling expenses with other congregations. It will be up to the TM whether he accepts the offer, but usually it is appreciated, and it can be a great opportunity for you to build deeper relationships with other churches in your area.

There are certain traveling expenses which you are not expected to cover, but you may choose to do so. For example, if the TM wants to bring along several traveling companions, you will need to decide whether you are willing and able to cover the additional cost. If you cannot, be honest and say, "I am concerned about the extra responsibilities we will have because of the individuals you want to bring with you. Our church is not in a financial position to handle the extra people. We want to bless you, but we do not feel good about the extra individual(s) whom you want to bring along. Is there some other arrangement you could make?" Be honest and then put the decision back on the TM.

As a TM, I will sometimes ask larger churches to pay for the flight of my wife or one traveling companion. I personally believe I am expecting too much in asking a smaller church to pay for the travel expenses of anyone other than myself. When a pastor willingly offers to fly my wife with me, I greatly appreciate it. Whether or not she is able to come at that time, the offer is still nice. When I bring my children along, I expect the host church to provide a place for them to sleep, but I usually pay their transportation myself.

Housing and food expenses are the responsibility of the host church for the length of the stay of the TM while ministering. If the TM is staying in a home with a member of the church, then the host should be instructed to take good care of their guest(s), and the church should offer to help the congregational member with the cost of food or extras. If the TM is staying in a motel, the host church should make pre-arrangements with the motel. Do not make the TM show up at the motel and be expected to convince the desk clerk that the church is going to cover the charge. The room should be ready and waiting.

Concerning the love offering or honorarium which is to be given to the TM, there are many different practices, depending upon the traditions of the church or denomination. Some churches, especially long-established congregations, have a policy for giving which has been determined by the church board. If that is the case, then policy must be followed, although the board should be aware of the real needs of TMs when making those policies.

If the church has a tradition of taking a special offering for the visiting speaker, then several suggestions should be made here. It is very common for small (under 100) to medium-sized churches (under 300) to give the entire offering to the TM, except for the Sunday morning offering. It is recognized that the Sunday morning offering is usually the largest and is essential to meet the expenses of the local church. Sometimes the pastor will take a second offering during the Sunday morning service which will be given to the TM; however, the people are to be instructed clearly what the purpose is for each offering.

The purpose of every offering should be stated *clearly*. This is especially important when more than one ministry is present. Each one knows that what they receive is at stake. Ears are open at the time the offering is taken. If you are having special meetings with a guest speaker and the offering is being taken to meet the needs of those meetings, then say that and use the money accordingly. If, however, you announce that the offering is "for the speaker and/or his ministry," do not use that money to cover the costs of the special meetings. All of it must go to the speaker.

This is a major area of offense between TMs and pastors. If you take an offering for the TM and that is what you say to the people, then all of the money must go to the speaker. Realize that you are under no obligation to take an offering exclusively for the speaker (unless, of course, you agreed with him ahead of time to do so), but if you do, stand by your words. If the people are told that the offering will go to the TM, the TM will expect all of it. If he feels that you kept part of it for the church, he may feel cheated, and he is justified in that feeling.

In order to keep things free of offense, there are specific things you can communicate with the TM. If an offering was taken and the people were told that it was for the TM, then tell the TM exactly how much was taken in the offering. Don't round off that amount to the nearest dollar. Set his mind at ease, and report the exact amount. You can bump the amount upward when you write a check to him, but you always should state what the actual amount was.

If, however, an offering is taken without mentioning that it will go to the TM, you do not need to tell. It is your business, unless you feel led to discuss it.

All this may seem a bit intense—perhaps even carnal. Please understand that the reason we are trying to communicate clearly is to give the enemy no opportunity to hurt or destroy. We are still human, and TMs can be under tremendous financial pressure at times.

I once spoke at an evening service of a church where the pastor took an offering which was supposed to be exclusively for me. After the service he asked me and several of his leaders to go out for dinner at a nice restaurant. I enjoyed the meal, but at the end he pulled out the envelope which held the offering of that night. He proceeded to pay for his own meal and the meals of everyone at the table, using the cash out of the envelope. Then he handed me the leftovers and bid me farewell. I doubt if he even knew how that hurt, for my wife was at home with three children and little food in the cupboard. Had I had a choice, I would not have used that money to buy dinner for his leaders or myself.

Although I never have been mistreated in any major way financially, I have several friends in ministry who have been. I have seen a root of bitterness form in their hearts against a certain pastor, and I have seen the pain in their eyes. Sometimes it is from a misunderstanding or miscommunication. Other times it is from wrong expectations of the TM. At all times it is unnecessary.

I try to keep in my heart the attitude that I will do my best to bless the people of God to whom I minister. I hope and expect the pastors to do their best to help me.

One more note worth mentioning is with regard to letting a TM take an offering. Some pastors prefer this because they do not like to take offerings. Keep in mind, however, that speakers who have much experience standing in front of people, usually know how to take large offerings. Some are anointed by God at it, while others have enough personal charisma and authority to stir the people to respond. The pastor must consider this and personally know the speaker before letting him take such an offering.

At times I will ask the pastor if I can take an offering to help his church meet their budget. This usually works wonderfully and the church is greatly blessed.

However, when a TM takes an offering for *his own* ministry, care must be exercised. If you trust the speaker because you have an ongoing relationship with him, and you feel led, then give him the opportunity to take an offering. In fact, I believe it is healthy for people to be stirred on occasion to give beyond the "practical." A spirit of liberality can be released among your people and it will not decrease the church's required provisions for the future. Rather, it will create a new freedom which will bless the church for weeks after the visiting minister has left. On the other hand, if your people have given beyond their abilities in preceding weeks, you need to guard them and not allow someone to come in and take advantage of their generosity. You know your people. Let them experience the blessings of giving, but protect them from abuse.

When it is finally time to give the TM a check for his labor, it is always best to make out a church check to the name of his ministry. Most TMs have an organization, corporation, or at least a bank account with a name other than their own. Anytime you give an individual a certain amount of money (in the US presently an amount over $599.00 per year), you are hiring them as a "contract laborer;" and, therefore, you must file the appropriate tax forms with the IRS at the end of the year. If, on the other hand, the TM is part of a non-profit corporation and you make the check out to the name of the corporation, then you are not required to report it. (Consult your accountant on these matters.)

Finally, make sure you give the check to him before he leaves. I will mention this again in later discussions, but for now let me say that TMs learn that checks not in hand when they leave tend to disappear or decrease in size. It is sad, but true. When a TM is present and the revival spirit is in the air, people want to return the blessing. However, one week later, after the one disgruntled person has complained to the pastor about the TM, and the hearts of the people are looking at clean-up of the building and normal work responsibilities, the heart of blessing fades. Out of sight, out of mind. A TM needs to be rewarded. Right after pouring out his life and being left physically and emotionally exhausted, he needs to know that you love him. Of course, your hug and prayer is nice, but your check is wonderful. Don't tell him the check is in the mail. He may *tell* you it is OK, but hurt may be left in his heart.

To the Traveling Minister,

"Don't quit your day job." This is a saying sometimes used to tell people who are considering a new career that it will not be easy, and that it may take an extended period to make it financially successful.

As I mentioned earlier, I slept in my car on many occasions when I first began traveling from church to church. Because my wife and I had three young children, it was especially difficult. Today it causes me pain to hear of some young zealot starting out in the traveling ministry while little children are still at home with mom. The last advice they want to hear is to keep working another job. They typically want to abandon all and "believe God." That is the attitude with which I started.

In the eyes of a pastor, that way of living is irresponsible. One of the pastor's primary jobs is to help sheep live responsibly before God. When a TM visits their church, but is "believing God" and under terrible financial stress at the same time, the pastor sees trouble. He sees a TM who is not taking care of his family. He concludes that that TM needs a pastor!

On one occasion while I was pastoring, a certain TM arrived at our church with a wife and several needy children. With all his heart he wanted to serve God on the road; however, his personal life was a mess, with one of his sons repeatedly stealing and in jail more than once. He arrived at the church unannounced, just expecting God to open the doors for his ministry. Unfortunately, or fortunately (depending how you look at it), I was a door that did not open.

Of course, God provides. Of course, believing God opens the provisions of heaven. Of course, God wants His people answering the call with total trust. But sometimes trust involves *tent making* as Paul did at times during his ministry (Acts 18:3). Working a secular job, while at the same time building a ministry, is sometimes necessary and according to God's will.

As I write these words, I am speaking against attitudes which I carried as I started out traveling. On several occasions when things got really tough, I held down several temporary jobs, such as driving a school bus, construction, washing cars, etc. Every time, I battled with the thought that I was backsliding because I was not out ministering. Today, as I look back, I wish I had worked more willingly at those jobs and others, while at the same time building the ministry.

Linda, my wife, also held down several temporary jobs during those first few years. Even though she carried most of the responsibility for the children, she was motivated strongly to get out and succeed. It caused quite a bit of tension between us—unnecessary tension. Forgive me, Lord.

Please hear this. If you are called to the traveling ministry, there is still time to fulfill that call. Do not think you have to do it all today. I once heard a very famous minister asked this question: "If you had to do it all over again, what would you do differently?" His answer was this: "I would go slower." I have to agree.

An attitude of being more relaxed and going more slowly applies to every area of finances in the traveling ministry. If you minister in a church while desperate for money, it will become evident. It may come out in your teaching, or in the relationships you try to build, or in the way you take offerings, or in the expectations you put on the local pastor. It causes trouble.

Now, I am not suggesting that you be uncaring or nonchalant about finances. No. You need to be businesslike and upfront. Talk openly with the pastor as the subject comes up. Let him know of your needs.

It took my wife and me about seven years of traveling before we became "more comfortable" financially. We had no previously opened doors nor denomination backing us. I made a lot of mistakes, and it would have taken less time if I had known then what I know now. There are a few TMs who make it financially right from the start, but there are very few. I tell you of our struggles so you can have a more realistic view.

Our book sales supplement our income, but that, too, took an extended period. We could not find a publishing company willing to purchase my first books, so we had to pay for the printing ourselves. We have marketed those books through the mail and through our traveling ministry, setting up a table at the back of most churches at which we minister. The truth is, however, that we gave away almost all of the first thousand books we printed just to get the message out. After about two years, the first book began selling and at least paying for itself.

Teaching tapes also can supplement one's income, but you don't want to look like a salesman. There is nothing more disconcerting than a TM who spends half his ministry time trying to sell his products. Of course, mentioning of one's books and tapes from the pulpit will release much favor on the sales table. However, you will be disappointed if you are selling teaching items solely for the purpose of making money. You must have a higher purpose of putting good teachings into the hands of the people. Then you will not be disappointed and finances will be a byproduct.

After about seven years on the road, my wife and I raised partners to help support our ministry through prayer and financial giving. We have continued to mail a monthly letter to encourage and stay in touch with our partners. It takes constant vision-sharing to keep partners interested in your work. However, it is true: *Vision plus people equals resources.* As I tell the ministers to whom I give financial instruction, "Don't beg; share vision."

Having people support you is especially important when you start ministering in third-world countries. When you go to the poorer regions of the world, you end up paying for your travel, food, housing, and everything else. It is expensive. However, Christian men and women want to help. There are thousands of godly people who want to support worthwhile ministries. If you want to learn how to do it effectively, you should seek advice from an experienced TM.

Whatever money comes through your hands, you need to keep records—accurate records. Be responsible concerning the requirements of the government. Find someone to help you. Do not keep all your financial dealings to yourself. You need to be accountable to someone—and not just your spouse. You need another person with a careful eye to see that the checkbook balances and that the bills that come in the mail are paid.

For the first few years, I managed our finances myself. Of course, there was very little money and it required little work. However, I kept accurate records. When a traveling ministry is small, it is typical for money simply to go wherever it is needed the moment it comes in. Whatever is left over ends up in the hands of the TM and his family. There are no set budgets during that time. However, as things grow, a TM needs to receive a set salary from a separate ministry account. Records need to be kept of where every dollar goes. The government is watching, but more important, God is watching. Be faithful with the small amounts and He will bless with greater amounts.

There are many details concerning record-keeping and budgeting, and we cannot address them all here. The best thing for a TM to do is to talk to a TM who has been in ministry for some time and see how they are doing it. And/or have an accountant advise the TM. This is not as difficult as it may sound at first. In most large-to-medium-sized churches, there is someone wise enough to give good advice on these subjects. Many pastors have dealt enough with church finances to answer most questions. However, a TM also should talk to a person with specific information about the traveling ministry.

Be honest with every penny. When you sell a book or tape, put the money in the right place. Don't sneak out a dollar here or there for a meal. It won't be blessed. When someone gives you a "Pentecostal handshake," that is, a handshake with a few dollars passed along, make sure the money goes where it is supposed to. When the pastor hands you that check and thanks you for your ministry, treat the gift as holy unto the Lord. People's hearts are behind that gift. They believe in you. They have invested themselves in your work. Prove yourself faithful to them and to God.

Also, it is important that you continue giving to God's work. Sometimes TMs rationalize to themselves that they are giving "everything to God," and, therefore, they don't tithe or give in any methodical manner. That is a mistake. I have seen repeatedly that when a minister governs his finances in a careless manner, he will not be blessed. Give a tithe to whomever is feeding you spiritually. I also like to plant seed offerings in the local churches at which I minister. Even the Levites tithed in the Old Testament times. You, too, be a priest in submission to God.

This is the road to greater blessings.

Chapter 5

Authority and Accountability

Different churches have established different types of authority relationships with different TMs. There are some TMs who are employed by a specific denomination, and they come into a local church carrying the authority of that denomination. There are other churches which look up to some outside leader, such as an apostolic figure, and that local church has submitted itself to the oversight of that TM. However, in the vast majority of cases, the local minister has authority over the local congregation; therefore, the visiting minister must submit to the authority of the local pastor.

This must be emphasized and stated clearly. If there is no pre-arranged, pre-agreed-upon relationship to the contrary, the TM must come into the local church with a submissive, helpful attitude.

There are some TMs who believe they have received a God-ordained mandate to enter a local church and demand submission. I confess that when I first began traveling, I had this attitude to some degree, but since then I have learned how authority works.

Where does authority originate? We understand that every authority that exists has been established by God (Rom. 13:1). When God spoke over Adam and Eve, "Fill the earth and subdue it," He imparted into mankind the authority to govern (Gen. 1:28). Whenever people take their individual authorities and unite in heart, they develop a *corporate authority* which is greater than the sum of their individual authorities. This is true in any situation of life—business, family, government, etc. Whenever people join together, they establish corporate authority.

In the local church, authority is the result of people committing to work together. The pastor gains authority as the people learn to trust him. As the years go by, commitments are made deeper in their hearts. As new leaders arise around the senior minister, authority grows. God honors the covenants made between people, and He backs the authority which results.

When a TM steps into the local church, he is stepping into an established authority structure—one that has taken years to develop—one which has resulted from people's heart commitments to each other.

When a pastor invites a TM to minister, he is opening up his doors of authority to influence his people. That is a privilege and an honor. The TM must respect it. To come on the scene and attempt to take that church in a different direction than it has been going would be to undermine God-backed authority. It is not right.

The TM is, therefore, accountable first and foremost to the local church leadership where he is ministering. If he is asked not to minister on certain subjects, then he must respect that. If he is asked to limit his speaking time to 30 minutes, he needs to obey and not make an excuse such as, "God isn't done yet." There is no excuse. Authority exists and it must be respected.

I have learned over the years that if I really want to change a local church, I must influence the pastor and his leaders. This takes confidence in my own calling and ministry. When I first started out in the traveling ministry, I sometimes directed my energy at the handful of hungry, easily-influenced zealots sitting in every church. I did not believe in my heart that I actually could change the leadership, so I aimed at the younger ones who seemed to receive more easily from me. What I learned over those first few years is that I was causing incredible confusion. What I was doing was unfair, because I was creating dissatisfaction in the hearts of a few, which stirred them to fight against their leadership for weeks after my visit.

As I explained in Chapter 3, a form of spiritual adultery was being committed. A few people would grab onto my words and anointing to such an extent that they would, in a sense, become one with me. But a few days later I was gone, offering no on-going relationship or day-by-day support, as only the local church can provide. Such a ministry takes on the characteristics of a man committing adultery everywhere he goes, producing children, but taking no responsibility in caring for those children. It is wrong.

On the other hand, if a TM imparts his spiritual strength and anointing to the whole church, and especially the leadership, then the whole church benefits and grows.

Young TMs usually do not have the confidence in their own calling to influence leaders. Or they envision in their heart the church leadership as rebellious and unwilling to change. In their misconception and lack of faith in their own calling, they take a ministry opportunity to change only those whom they feel strong enough to influence.

Let me speak to TMs at this point. I can see the error of spiritual adultery because I was guilty of it, all the time thinking I was doing God's will. The truth is that most leaders in most churches are hungry to grow and change. You may be intimidated by them, but in reality they are in the ministry because their heart has been to serve God. In order to produce lasting change, you must believe in them and in your own anointing to influence them.

There are other difficulties and problems which may arise from the ministry of a TM, and this is the very reason why pastors often are concerned about TMs being accountable to someone. We already have stated that the TM is accountable and must be in submission to the local church leadership where he is ministering. However, local pastors also expect the TM to be accountable to some other outside leader. Pastors want someone whom they can call to check on a certain TM prior to or following a ministry time. Is this valid and how should it be worked out?

Many TMs are licensed ministers with and/or belong to a certain organization or denomination. If that is the case, then a pastor can contact the headquarters of that organization. Other TMs have established their own ministry, and they function independently. It is the second group for which most concern is raised.

I must admit that I am one of them, so I will answer this question from an insider's perspective. Through the years of pastoring and traveling, I have been licensed and associated with various Christian organizations; however, at present I head my own non-profit corporation with my own staff and headquarters. This arrangement provides many advantages. When I was associated with certain Christian groups, I was expected to minister primarily in those groups, which is very limiting. Now that my ministry has grown and is well accepted, I can minister to the larger Body of Christ, crossing denominational lines freely.

No matter how influential a certain TM may be, he needs to be in open fellowship with other leaders. Those relationships must be the kind in which open communication is carried on—even sins must be confessed. Honesty and integrity must reign. The people involved must not be only those already in submission to the leader, but they must stand shoulder-to-shoulder, ready to confront and speak into each others' lives.

I do not trust TMs who are isolated and outside such relationships. I do not believe a pastor should allow in his church any TM who has separated himself from the larger Body of Christ. Every pastor should be confident in asking the TM, "With whom are you in close relationship?" The answer to that question reveals much about the person and offers to the pastor someone with whom he can communicate in case problems arise.

Chapter 6

Traveling Companions

TMs pick up helpers along the way, and some of those helpers can cause problems. A few pointers are worth giving here.

In every church there are at least two or three wide-eyed zealots strongly attracted to the TM's anointing. They would give anything for the opportunity to travel with the TM and minister, catch the mantle and/or share the glory. After traveling for a few years, every TM learns that such hungry ones are "a dime a dozen." I do not say this to belittle them in any way, for I know they are precious in God's sight. But I word it this way in order to help the TM face reality. There always will be people who wish they could share in a ministry that appears anointed and blessed by God. Therefore, you will have to learn how to say, "No."

You cannot bring a carload of people with you. It is unfair to expect a local church, especially a small-to-medium-sized one, to provide beds and food for all of them. In most cases the church is asking *you* to come, not you and two, three, four, or more others.

three, four, or more others.

The presence of tagalongs not only puts a financial stress upon a local church, but it also hinders the communication which needs to take place between the TM and the local leaders. This is one of the most important functions of a TM. In fact, in many places I go to minister, I believe I accomplish more during my hour or two of talking privately with the pastor and other leaders than I do during several hours of up-front, public ministry. If, however, I have a traveling companion always sitting next to me, the pastor will rarely share his heart and real concerns.

This is not true when my traveling companion is my wife, because the pastor usually sees her as a part of me, and she actually opens up tremendous doors of communication, especially to the pastor's wife and other female leaders. However, other traveling companions typically fit into a servant role, coming along to help me. Of course, we want to treat all people with love and respect, but it is a reality that people communicate on different levels, and the presence of an outsider can shut down completely any deeper communication. When that happens, I feel that I have missed out on the most important part of my ministry while visiting a church.

I have had several different traveling companions during the years, and, among other things, I have learned that I always need to explain this dynamic to them. Carefully and with all the grace I can, I have to teach them to give me and the local leaders some space—to excuse themselves from our presence or at least to resist the urge of injecting their thoughts into our conversation. During that time the companions often feel put out or put down, but this is a reality with which they must deal.

One of the problems in choosing traveling companions is in finding the right type of person. Of course, my first choice is my wife, but because we began the traveling ministry with three small children, it was not always convenient for her to leave home. Now that our children are older, she is able to travel more freely; I also love to take turns bringing each of the children along.

When it is a non-family person I choose to bring along, I want to have someone who actually will help me. That is more difficult than it sounds. The people who most want to go with me are those who want someday to have a ministry similar to mine. That causes a problem. When you have a person whose heart is aimed at future ministry, they usually have a difficult time doing the natural, practical duties. When you are up front praying over people, they do not want to be in the back watching the book table. When you are meeting the pastor, the last thing they want to do is carry in the luggage from the car. When you need time alone to pray, they feel pushed out of the most important time of your life. And finally, when they do catch your anointing and learn how to minister, they leave to start their own ministry.

Of course, we want more people to go out and succeed in ministry. Plus, I have a heart to raise sons in the faith, as with Elijah and Elisha. However, I also have a job to do and I need help at times. This may sound harsh, but after a few years on the road, I began praying for God to send me helpers who "had no desire to minister up front." That is right. I have learned to appreciate even more the support ministries whose only desire is to help.

If I bring along a non-family member with me today, I am aware of the dynamics in our relationships. If they are there to grow in their own ministry, it is great, but I have no misconceptions about where their heart is. More frequently, I prefer to bring along individuals gifted by God to fit into the helps ministry, because that is where they always will be most happy and fulfilled. Sometimes I will bring along with me a person who has been helping with our work at the home office. I want them to know what is going on out in the field. It is partly a reward for their faithful service to the ministry. It also helps them to keep their own sense of purpose while continuing month after month reproducing tapes, mailing books, answering letters, or doing some other naturally oriented job. Whoever I bring—if I bring anyone at all—I make sure that they are not a burden to the local church, and that they do not hinder my personal communication with the church leadership.

Chapter 7

Spiritual, Physical, and Emotional Exhaustion

This last chapter is mostly for the benefit of the TM, but a pastor also can apply the principles to his own life and learn here how to help TMs in perhaps their greatest area of defeat.

Ministry can be exhausting and stressful. The pastorate has it own problems, but the TM deals even more with the results of great expenditures of energy. They are expected to be exciting and full of the power of God. They may go from one meeting to another, traveling through several time zones, and not resting for weeks. They often eat large, quick meals at restaurants and get very little normal, physical exercise. They sit motionless in a car or airplane, then walk in front of a large crowd where they explode with enthusiasm. They cannot sleep in their own bed, and during a series of meetings get very little rest. It is not a healthy lifestyle and opens the door for serious problems.

Through the years I have learned some things that have helped me.

First, we must recognize that the human

body has the ability to perform at different levels of productivity. At its most active level, there is what some have called "a flight or fight mechanism" in which the adrenaline flows, the brain activities accelerate, and the functions unnecessary for immediate action shut down. God has created us this way so that we might handle emergency situations, but we also can recognize similar activities of the body kicking in when a minister stands in front of a crowd of people.

The adrenaline flows, muscles tense, and the heart beats faster. When I preach, I often can feel the size of my neck expanding, and a tie that was comfortable at the start of a meeting will be at least an inch too tight by the end. Many internal bodily functions change. A minister who was feeling weak or ill before a meeting may feel fully healed and refreshed as he stands before the masses. We can give credit to the anointing of God, but we also need to recognize real physiological changes going on in the body.

For example, digestive functions slow down in the intensity of the hour. Compounded by long periods of travel and constant changes in diet, TMs frequently experience gastrointestinal problems. Then after a series of meetings, their physical bodies may crave food to restore lost resources. Overeating and foods too rich in fat can be a serious problem.

What is the answer? Simply to be aware of these stresses. Extra care should be taken to exercise and eat healthfully. It may be convenient to eat a meal after each evening meeting, but it is not always healthful. If you are going to last at this ministry for the long run, you have to take care of your body.

Consider also the activity of your brain. Have you ever been in a car wreck, and just before impact you watched other obstacles coming at your vehicle? It seems like time is slowing down. Often each second is crammed full of hundreds of bits of information. What is happening? Your thought processes actually are accelerating, looking for solutions in the emergency situation.

Similar thought acceleration can happen when a person is put in front of a crowd of people. This enables them to think fast, make decisions, and teach with more command and authority. Often, ministers have learned to trigger these functions subconsciously by putting themselves in panic situations. For example, before a meeting a speaker may be thinking, "Oh no, I have nothing to preach! What am I going to say? God hasn't given me anything." An experienced minister subconsciously may put himself through a specific progression of thoughts which automatically trigger the flight or fight mechanisms of the mind.

Yes, we can call all of this the anointing of God, and I believe in the anointing, but it is time we face some physiological realities here.

When the human brain accelerates, thoughts can be sorted out much more rapidly, and the person at the front may be thinking six times faster than the person in the audience. However, the thought patterns seem to course through the nervous system by different avenues. Well-worn patterns of thought may pour out in words at a rapid rate. Sayings that have been used time and time again may flow like a river. But also the thought patterns seem not to take the slower, more methodical paths used in normal communication. As a consequence, things spoken are sometimes not thought out completely. Or at the height of excitement, stories may be exaggerated, numbers may increase, and the truth may be stretched. This is not intentional and no God-fearing preacher wants to exaggerate, but in reality they sometimes lose control

I even have known some ministers who seem to outright lie after their physiological functions are so accelerated. We can call it the devil and try all we want to cast him out, but I am asking you to also take a look at this problem from a practical, natural point of view. It is not always the devil. Just as a trapped animal will respond aggressively, and sometimes irrationally, so also a human being may not have control of himself to the same degree when his natural functions are accelerated.

I am not making excuses for the evangelist who exaggerates. We sometimes jokingly use the terminology, "evangelastically speaking." This is wrong and there is no excuse. Understanding this problem, however, can help TMs avoid it, and also can assist pastors in dealing with TMs who yield to it (not to mention pastors them-selves who sometimes fail in this area).

It is not just the stretching of truth about which we are concerned here, and I do not want to imply that every TM will have problems in this area. There are other areas in which related problems may appear.

For example, after a meeting, a TM may be so exhausted that he is open for emotional and spiritual attack. It is very common for TMs to go through battles of inferiority and defeat after ministering. We can read how the prophet Elijah hid in a cave after defeating the false prophets of Baal (I Kings 18:20-19:14). Elijah wanted to give up in the ministry, and he cried out to God saying that there was no one else serving Him. Jonah, too, pleaded with God to end his life—after he led the entire city of Nineveh in revival (Jonah 4). We could say that they just fell into self-pity, and, indeed, that is exactly what it sounds like, but it does not provide us with the answers we need.

It is not just a spiritual problem. In both Elijah's and Jonah's cases, God sent specific nat-ural aids—food and the shade of a tree—to help them rest and be restored physically. Scientific studies have been made in modern times that show actual chemical depletions in the brain after emotionally strenuous periods. Until those chemicals are restored, it is impossible for the individual to maintain healthy, positive thought patterns. It does not matter how much a certain minister prays or seeks God, they usually will not find freedom from negative thoughts until some healing time or rest has taken place.

Yes, of course, the devil may take opportunity through the weaknesses of the flesh. Prayer actually may be what is necessary, and, indeed, there will be times when a person can be set free instantly from thoughts of defeat and faithlessness by rebuking the devil in Jesus' name. However, there are also times when rest and relaxation is needed. God provided this natural answer for both Elijah and Jonah.

I know several TMs, including myself, who at times have received medical treatment for difficulties related to exhaustion. It is not an embarrassment to have to admit needing help, but it is an embarrassment not to get help when you need it. We need all ministers to face the problems we are discussing and approach them with a desire to help.

One thing a pastor can do for each and every TM that ministers at his church is to tell him that his ministry has been appreciated greatly. Most of the TMs that I personally know go through terrible times of self-doubt shortly after they finish a series of intensive meetings. They may not let the pastor or anyone else know because they feel obligated to appear strong, but inside they often battle with thoughts of failure. In fact, every negative thing they ever have done in their lifetime can be on the forefront of their mind for several days after a great revival. Pastoral reassurance at such times is very powerful. Please, pastors, don't hold back your words, even if the TM acts confident and stable.

Second, a pastor can make sure the TM receives a check for his ministry immediately after completing his work. This may sound greedy or evil, but please do not take it that way. The laborer is worthy of his wages, and it really does help to have something real and tangible in hand to reassure one that his labor was not in vain. In my own ministry, even though all the money which comes in goes to our organization, and not directly to me, I must admit that a check to take home when it is all over helps me.

When a TM is finished with an extensive ministry time, he is often open for other forms of attack as well. It is at that time that some fall into sexual temptations. That does not mean they should be watched over like a hawk. However, a married TM who is traveling alone should be allowed to telephone his spouse every day and to go home as soon as a series of meetings are over. Don't try to talk them into staying and hanging around for a few days afterward, unless they request it.

One of my pet peeves is having people come for ministry after I am completely exhausted. Of course, I wish I were like Jesus, loving to the end, but I am weak. On more than one occasion, I have had the people who are driving me to the airport hang on me for some last parting prophecy or prayer. Some ministers are social to the end, but personally, I give it all during the meetings and want to return home unhindered when I am done. Like a horse returning to the stable, I am on the run.

People also like to pray for the TM after he has finished his time of ministry. Some groups even make it a custom to lay hands on the TM and impart blessings before he leaves. Different leaders feel differently about this, but I do not like it. When I have expended all of my energy, the last thing I want is people whom I do not know laying hands on me. I don't mind the senior minister laying on hands and/or leading the congregation in prayer for me. Also, I appreciate the prayers of any of the saints, if they quietly pray without laying hands on me or capturing my time and remaining energy. But the laying-on of hands is a powerful spiritual operation, and we are warned in the Scripture not to lay hands on anyone too casually or readily (I Tim. 5:22). I am careful how and when I lay my hands on people for spiritual impartations, and I appreciate the same from others.

In fact, I expect local pastors to protect me from the well-meaning, yet unknowing Christian who wants to come and minister over me. Most people do not realize how trying it can be to have a congregational member come up and ask the TM at the end of a meeting, "Can I pray for you?" It would sound downright rude and arrogant for a TM to say no, so he usually submits. But what is really happening is that the TM is working, and working very hard, with the eyes of a large crowd still on him, many still hoping to receive ministry. The TM has to stop his work, lose whatever charge of the meeting he had, and allow the congregational member to practice prayer on him. I do not mean to sound disrespectful, but pastors should not allow their congregational members to put a TM in such a position. Of course, such prayer will teach the congregation that everyone is able to pray, and that even the TM needs prayer, but that is not the time.

I have signals that I have worked out with my staff and/or those who travel with me at various times. When I make the signal, they know someone needs to "rescue me." Sometimes it is a prayer-person that I need rescuing from. Other times it is a lonely woman who has no one with whom to talk. Still other times it is the zealot with a pet doctrine that he tries to unload on every visiting minister. Or it may be the person who recently signed up for a multi-level marketing scheme, and they think I should be on their downline. When I am standing in front of a church at the end of meeting and any one of these precious people corner me, I signal for a helper to come up and say, "Harold, we need you right now outside." I then excuse myself and follow them out the door. I do not like to be rude, but I have been doing this long enough to have learned how to protect myself.

That is what it takes—learning one's limits and not going beyond or letting others take advantage of you. I know how many people I can prophesy over and still have enough energy to get out of bed the next day. I know now how many meetings I can hold and still be in love with God when I am done. I know how much my physical body can take. If I unwittingly go over my limits, I try to allow myself to rest under an extra amount of grace for the days following. I work hard at remembering that God loves me during those down times. It works, but it has taken a long time to develop this more relaxed and confident lifestyle.

Closing Comments

While ministering at a successful church in California, the pastor boldly said to me, "Help me build my church!" That was a new thought to me. To be honest, when I began in the traveling ministry I was on a crusade to serve God and carry forth the message He had put on my heart. It really did not occur to me that I was to help pastors build their local churches.

After several years on the road, I came to a place of defeat, feeling I had failed God and not knowing what I was doing. Ever been there? I wondered if God had left me, and I seemed to lose track of my purpose for even ministering. My prayer changed during that time from, "Let's change the world," to "Please let me help Your church." I still want to change the world, but my heart changed during that period of disillusionment—or enlightenment—depending on how you want to look at it.

I once asked a gathering of pastors, "If you could tell traveling ministers one thing, what would it be?" The most common responses revolved around wanting more personal relationship with the TMs, rather than their speeding into town, preaching, and then zipping back out. They wanted to be friends. There's another new thought.

Appendix A

The following four pages are informational sheets which the traveling minister may fill out for the local church before arriving.

To be Completed by the Visiting Minister

Name _____

Phone # _____

Address or place of contact _____

_____

_____

E-mail _____

Transportation:

Driving? Yes _____ No _____

Flying? Yes _____ No _____

    Are you renting a car?   Yes _____ No _____

    Need to be picked up at the airport?

                        Yes _____ No _____

    Arrival:

    Date _____ Airport _____ Airline _____

    Flight #_____ Time _____

    Departure:

    Date _____ Airport _____ Airline _____

    Flight #_____ Time _____

Do you need rides to and from meetings?

                        Yes_____ No _____

If you are driving, do you need a map or instructions
on how to get to the church? hotel? or elsewhere?

_____

Should these directions be available when you arrive
or should we send them to you before you come?

_____

Accommodations:

Do you prefer to stay in a hotel or a home with church
members?

_____

_____

Food:
Do you prefer to eat in a restaurant or home?

_____

Preferences for:
  Breakfast _____
  Lunch _____
  Dinner _____
Are there any foods that you especially do not
  enjoy?_____
Are there any foods that you very much
  enjoy?_____
Special dietary requirements

_____

After an evening meeting, if time allows, do you like
to get something to eat? Yes _____ No _____
  With others? Yes _____ No _____
  With whom?_____

Financial Concerns:
Do you have a set amount required for your ministry
time with us? _____
If you are flying, would you like us to obtain the ticket
or reimburse you for the cost?_____
What are your travel expenses?
  Flight cost?_____
  Driving?_____
  Food?_____
  Other?_____
To whom would you like the check(s) made out?

_____

If the check is to be made out to you or an unincorpo-
rated ministry, what is your social security or federal
I.D. number?

_____

Traveling Companions:
Is your spouse coming with you? Yes_____ No _____
Are any of your children coming with you?
  Yes _____ No _____
  If so, what are their names and ages?

  _____

  _____

Would you like any special arrangements made for your family members?

  _____

  _____

  _____

Others traveling with you? Yes _____ No _____
  If so, what are their names and relationship to you?_____

  _____

  Do they have special needs?

  _____

Total number traveling with you?_____
Any special arrangements that need to be made?

  _____

  _____

  _____

Book or Tape Sales:
Will you be bringing books, tapes, or other items to be sold?
  Books?_____ Tapes?_____ Other? _____
Will you need a table set up or other facility arrangements made?_____
Will you need someone to help with your sales table?_____
Related information?_____

_____

Miscellaneous:
Before meetings, do you prefer:
  To be alone?_____ Pray with a group?_____
  Be with other church leaders?_____
At the end of a meeting do you prefer:
  To minister as long as necessary? _____
  Visit with the people?_____
  Be escorted out?_____
Are there any ministry aids which you would like available?
  Musical instruments?_____
  Overhead projector? _____
  Anointing Oil?_____
  Other?_____
Do you like something to drink while ministering?
  Water?_____ Coffee?_____ Other?_____

Is there anything we can tell your host to make your stay more pleasant? _____
_____
_____
_____

Other helpful information or requests?
_____
_____
_____
_____
_____
_____
_____

Appendix B

The following two pages are informational sheets which the church may send to the traveling minister in order to confirm to him or her the arrangements which have been made.

Confirmation and Information
for Your Forthcoming Visit

Arrival:
_____We understand that you will be driving in and
arriving at
(date) _____
(time) _____
_____We will have (name) _____
pick you up
at the _____airport
(date) _____
(time) _____ AM or PM
flight # _____

Accommodations:
You will be staying
at the home of _____
at the motel/hotel called _____
or_____
When you arrive, your room will be reserved
under the name of _____

Ministry time:
The topic(s) around which we want your ministry
centered are:

_____
_____
_____

You are scheduled to minister at:
    Date   Time   Location

_____
_____
_____
_____

The approximate number of people to whom you will be ministering is _____

We ask that your ministry be limited to:
_____

Other requests and expectations:
_____
_____
_____

Attire—The Church leaders will be dressed:
Formally _____
Causally _____
Recreationally _____
Other _____

Directions:
Enclosed on a separate sheet is a map or directions:
     _____ to the church
     _____ to the hotel
     _____ to the home where you will be staying
     _____ other _____

Departure:
_____We understand that you will be leaving:
    date _____
    time _____ AM or PM
_____We will have (name) _____
    give you a ride
    to the _____ airport,
    (date) _____
    (time)_____ AM or PM
    flight # _____

Let us mail copies of this book to pastors and traveling ministers whom you know.

For a current price or to place an order by phone, call:

1-800-308-5837 within the USA
509-248-5837 from outside the USA

or write to:

**Winepress Publishing
P.O. Box 10653
Yakima, WA 98909-1653 USA**

MasterCard/VISA accepted.

E-mail:winepress@nwinfo.net
http://www.grmi.org/ministry/winepress/

Developing a Prosperous Soul
Vol. I: How to Overcome a Poverty Mind-set
Vol. II: How to Move into God's Financial Blessings

There are fundamental changes you can make in the way you think which will release God's blessings. This is a balanced look at God's promises with practical steps you can take to step into financial freedom. It is time for Christians to recapture the financial arena.

Spiritual Realities

(Now five volumes* of a seven volume series)

Here they are—the series explaining the spiritual world from a Christian perspective. In this series Harold R. Eberle deals with issues such as:

- What exists in the spiritual world
- Discerning things in the spirit
- Interpretation of dreams
- Angelic and demonic visitations
- Activities of witches, psychics and New Agers
- The Christian perspective of holistic medicine
- Spiritual impartations and influences between people
- Understanding supernatural phenomena from a Biblical perspective

- How people access that realm
- Out-of-the-body experiences
- What the dead are experiencing

Now you can have answers to the questions you always have wanted to ask about the supernatural world and spiritual phenomena.

Vol. I: The Spiritual World and How We Access It
Vol. II: The Breath of God in Us
Vol. III: Escaping Dualism

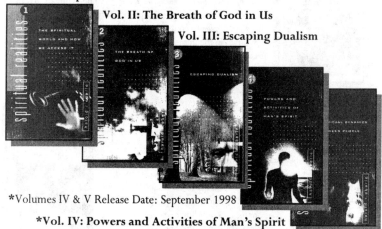

*Volumes IV & V Release Date: September 1998

*Vol. IV: Powers and Activities of Man's Spirit

*Vol. V: Spiritual Dynamics Between People

People Are Good

Harold R. Eberle is stirring up controversy with this one. Furthering the present reformation within the Church this book will cause a major paradigm shift in your mind. It will challenge fundamental beliefs, yet set Christians free and rejoicing. After reading this book you will look at life differently—more positively, with more hope and more realistically. You never will be the same.

You Shall Receive Power

Moving Beyond Pentecostal & Charismatic Theology
God's Spirit will fill you in measures beyond what you are experiencing presently. This is not about Pentecostal or Charismatic blessings. There is something greater. It is for all Christians and it will build a bridge between those Christians who speak in tongues and those who do not. It is time for the whole Church to take a fresh look at the work of the Holy Spirit in our individual lives. This book will help you. It will challenge you, broaden your perspective, set you rejoicing, fill you with hope, and leave you longing for more of God.

Dear Pastors and Traveling Ministers,

Here is a manual to help pastors and traveling ministers relate and minister together effectively. Topics are addressed such as finances, authority, ethical concerns, scheduling,.... In addition to dealing with real-life situations, an appendix is included with very practical worksheets to offer traveling ministers and local pastors a means to communicate with each other. Pastors and traveling ministers can make their lives and work much easier simply by reading this manual.